☑ **W9-BWF-391**

DATE			

EXPERIMENTS WITH COLORS

A TRUE BOOK®

by

Salvatore Tocci

Children's Press®
A Division of Scholastic Inc.

New York Toronto London Auckland Sydney
Mexico City New Delhi Hong Kong
Danbury, Connecticut

Reading Consultant
Susan Virgilio

Science Consultant
Tenley Andrews

The photograph on the cover shows paint cans. The photograph on the title page shows colorful pastel chalks.

The author and publisher are not responsible for injuries or accidents that occur during or from any experiments. Experiments should be conducted in the presence of or with the help of an adult. Any instructions of the experiments that require the use of sharp, hot, or other unsafe items should be conducted by or with the help of an adult.

Library of Congress Cataloging-in-Publication Data

Tocci, Salvatore.
   Experiments with colors / by Salvatore Tocci.
      p. cm. (A true book)
   Includes bibliographical references and index.
   Contents: What do you see? — How do we see colors? — Experiment 1, Mixing the colors — Experiment 2, Separating the colors — Experiment 3, Turning blue — Why are things colored? — Experiment 4, Seeing colors in a different light — Experiment 5, Separating the colors in black — Experiment 6, Turning black and white into color — How can you color things? — Experiment 7, Coloring fabrics — Experiment 8, Printing colors — Fun with colors — Experiment 9, Naming the colors.
      ISBN 0-516-22785-8 (lib. bdg.)   0-516-27804-5 (pbk.)
      1. Color—Experiments—Juvenile literature. [1. Color—Experiments. 2. Experiments.] I. Title. II. Series.
   QC495.5 .T59 2003
   535.6'078—dc21
                                                                    2002015264

CHILDREN'S PRESS, and A TRUE BOOK®, and associated logos are trademarks and or registered trademarks of Scholastic Library Publishing. SCHOLASTIC and associated logos are trademarks and or registered trademarks of Scholastic Inc.
1 2 3 4 5 6 7 8 9 10 R 12 11 10 09 08 07 06 05 04 03

Contents

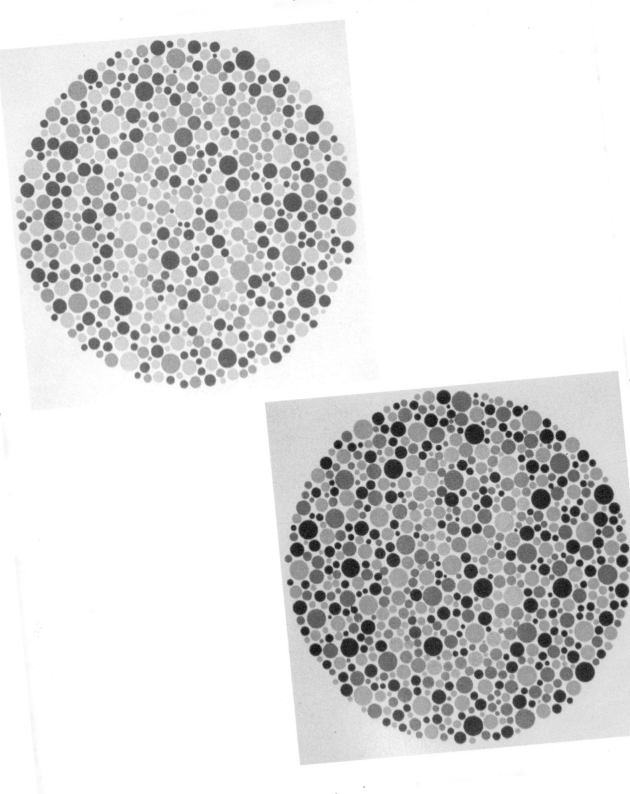

What Do You See?

What numbers do you see in the patterns of colored dots shown on the opposite page? If you see the numbers 6 and 8, you have normal color vision. Anyone who does not see these numbers is **colorblind** and cannot see the colors red and green.

This condition is called red-green colorblindness.

All babies are born color-blind. To a newborn baby, the world looks black and white. When a baby is about four months old, tiny structures at the back of the eyes develop and allow the baby to see the world in color. However, some of these structures may not develop normally. When this happens, a person may develop red-green colorblindness.

Now look at another pattern on the next page. How many colors do you see? The green and white squares are easy to see. But do you see two shades of pink, one darker than the other? You probably see one shade of pink surrounded by the green squares and a different shade of pink surrounded by the white squares.

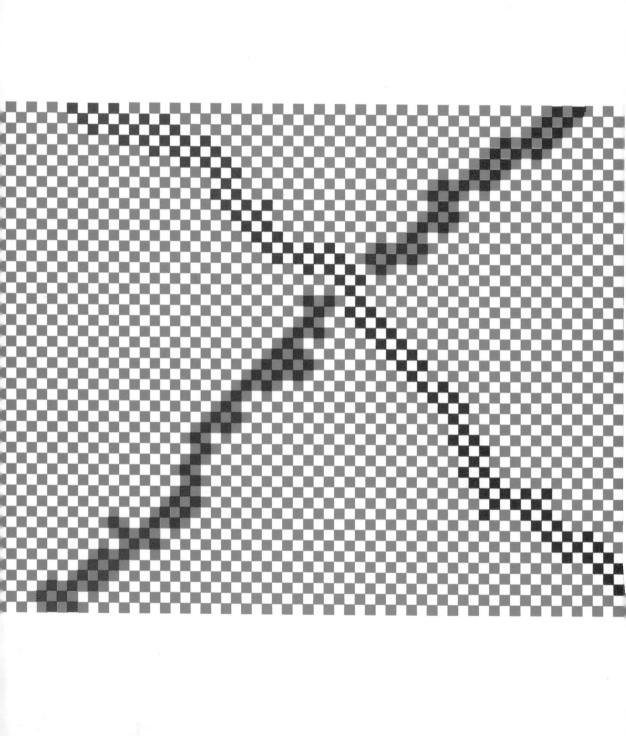

Actually, there is only one shade of pink in the picture. This is an example of an **optical illusion** that tricks most people's eyes. This optical illusion fools the tiny structures at the back of the eye that are responsible for seeing colors.

To learn more about colors, all you have to do is carry out the experiments in this book. You will also learn how to create your own optical illusion.

How Do You See Colors?

Your eyes are sensitive to only three colors: red, green, and blue. Yet you see many more than just these three colors. For example, you see blue, yellow, orange, and violet. You also see many shades of every color. In fact, the human eye can tell the

difference between almost
seven million different colors!
How can your eyes see so
many different colors?

Mixing the Colors

You will need:
- tape
- sheet of white paper
- two flashlights
- red, blue, and green cellophane
- darkened room or closet
- large round lid
- pencil
- small piece of white cardboard
- scissors
- ruler
- red, green, and blue felt-tip pens

Tape the white paper to a wall. Cover the lens of one flashlight with red cellophane. Cover the lens of the other flashlight with green cellophane. Darken the room. Shine both flashlights on the white paper. Slowly bring the lights together so that they overlap. What color do you see? Try overlapping other color combinations, such as red/blue and blue/green. What colors do you see?

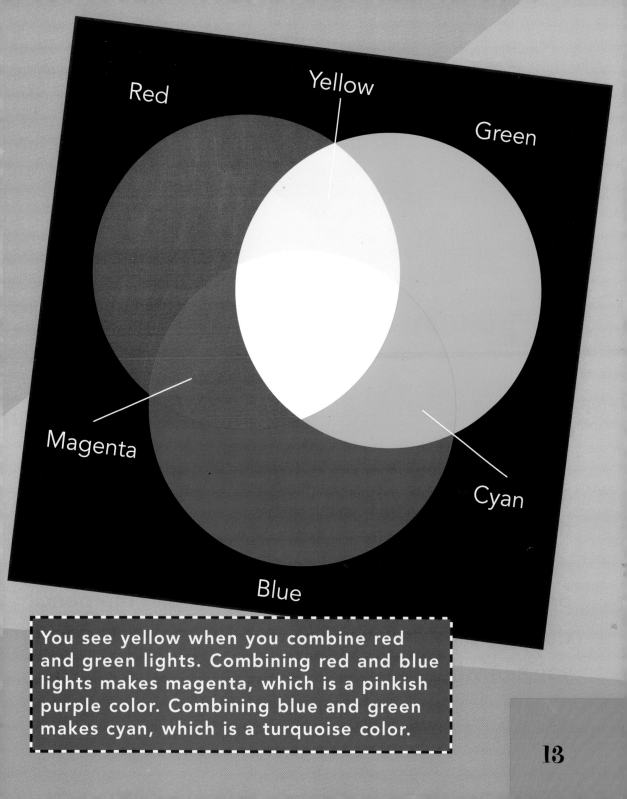

Red Yellow Green

Magenta

Cyan

Blue

You see yellow when you combine red and green lights. Combining red and blue lights makes magenta, which is a pinkish purple color. Combining blue and green makes cyan, which is a turquoise color.

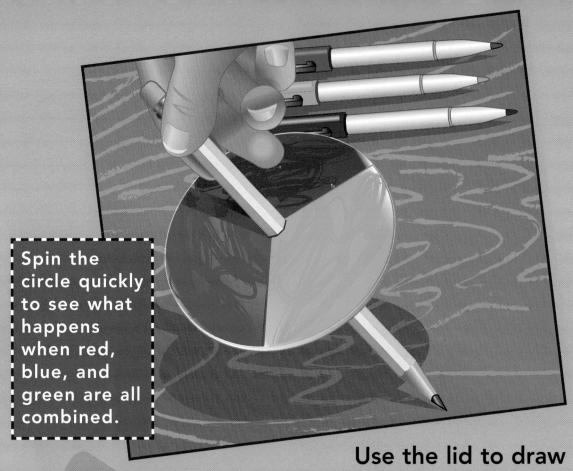

Spin the circle quickly to see what happens when red, blue, and green are all combined.

Use the lid to draw a circle on the cardboard. Cut out the circle. Use the pencil and ruler to divide the circle into three equal parts. Use the felt-tip pens to color each part of the circle a different color. Push the pencil through the center of the circle. What color do you see when you spin the circle like a toy top?

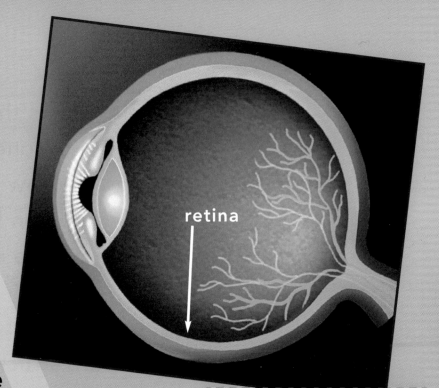

retina

There is an area in the back of the eye called the **retina**. The retina has three types of tiny structures called **cones**. Each type of cone is

The retina contains tiny structures called cones that allow you to see colors.

sensitive to a different color: red, blue, and green. When you look at a red object, only the "red" cones are struck by light. These cones send messages to your brain, which tells you that you are looking at a red object.

15

However, when light strikes the same number of "red" and "green" cones, you see yellow. This is why you see yellow when you bring together the red and green lights. If the light strikes one type of cone more than the other type, you will see a different shade of yellow. Therefore, the color you see depends on which cones are struck by light.

Why did the spinning circle with all three colors on it appear white? Spinning this circle sends light to the "red," "green," and "blue" cones. When all three types of cones are struck by light, you see all the colors combined. Combining the three colors makes white. Learn how you can separate even more colors that make up white.

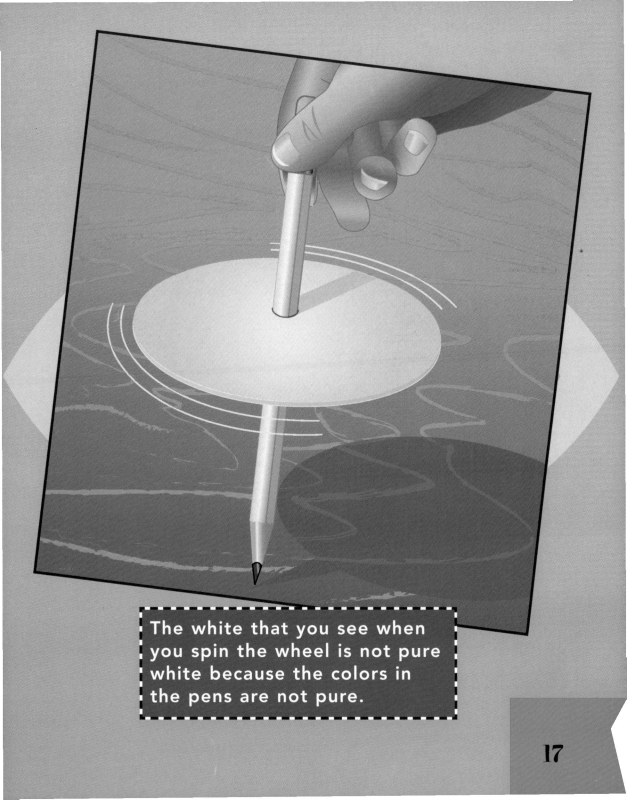

The white that you see when you spin the wheel is not pure white because the colors in the pens are not pure.

Separating the Colors

You will need:
- scissors
- ruler
- pencil
- sheet of white paper
- black plastic bag
- plastic plate with sections
- soap bubble solution
- straw

Cut a 4-inch by 8.5-inch (10-centimeter by 22-centimeter) strip from the sheet of white paper. Cut a 4-in. (10-cm) square from the black plastic bag. Wet the largest section of the plate with a little water. Cover this section with the black plastic square. Pour some bubble solution into another section of the plate. Dip the straw into the bubble solution. Blow a bubble onto the black plastic. Bend the strip of white paper around the bubble. Look closely at the bubble. What do you see?

If the bubble pops, blow another one until you can see different colors.

18

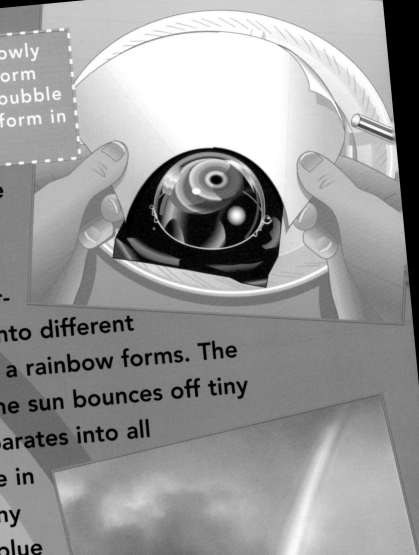

he colors will move slowly
round the bubble to form
ings. Just before the bubble
ops, a black dot will form in
the middle.

Light strikes the
surface of the bub-
ble. As the light
bounces off the sur-
face, it separates into different
colors. This is how a rainbow forms. The
white light from the sun bounces off tiny
raindrops and separates into all
the colors you see in
a rainbow. But why
do you see only blue
when the sky is clear?

The colors of a rainbow
include red, orange,
yellow, green, blue,
indigo, and violet. Can
you see all these colors
in this rainbow?

Turning Blue

You will need:
- sunny day
- sheet of white paper
- drinking glass
- straw
- milk

Place the white paper on a flat surface near a window so that the sun shines on it. Fill the glass with water and set it on the paper. Dip the straw into the milk. Place your finger on the open end of the straw. Hold the straw over the glass. Slowly release your finger to add a drop of milk to the water. Keep adding drops of milk until the water looks blue.

Practice until you can let one drop at a time fall from the straw.

The tiny milk drops in the glass act like the tiny dust particles that fill the air. When sunlight strikes the milk drops, they reflect, or bounce back, blue light. This is why the milk looks blue. When sunlight strikes the particles in the air during the day, they reflect blue light that is scattered through the sky. This is why the sky looks blue.

During the day, the sky is blue. When the sun sets, however, you see other colors such as pink. This happens because sunlight is scattered differently when the sun is low on the horizon.

Why Are Objects Colored?

The color of an object depends on what happens when light strikes it. You learned that the sky is blue because the dust particles in the air reflect blue light. However, sunlight is a mixture of the different colors you see in a rainbow. What happens to all the other colors in sun-light, such as red and yellow, that strike the dust particles in the air? All these colors are absorbed by the dust parti-cles, like water that gets soaked up by a sponge. Only blue light is reflected, making the sky look blue.

An object has the color it does because you see what-ever color of light it reflects. A fire engine looks red because

it reflects red light and
absorbs all the other colors.
But can something red ever
look like it is a different color?

Experiment 4

💡

Seeing Colors in a Different Light

You will need:
- scissors
- empty shoe box with cover
- tape
- blue or green cellophane
- small red object
- window or lamp

Cut a large, rectangular hole near one end of the cover of the shoe box. Cut a much smaller hole at the other end. Tape a piece of the colored cellophane over the large hole. Place the small red object inside the shoe box. Place the object so that it is under the cellophane when the cover is on the shoe box. Put the cover on the shoe box and set it near a window or lamp.

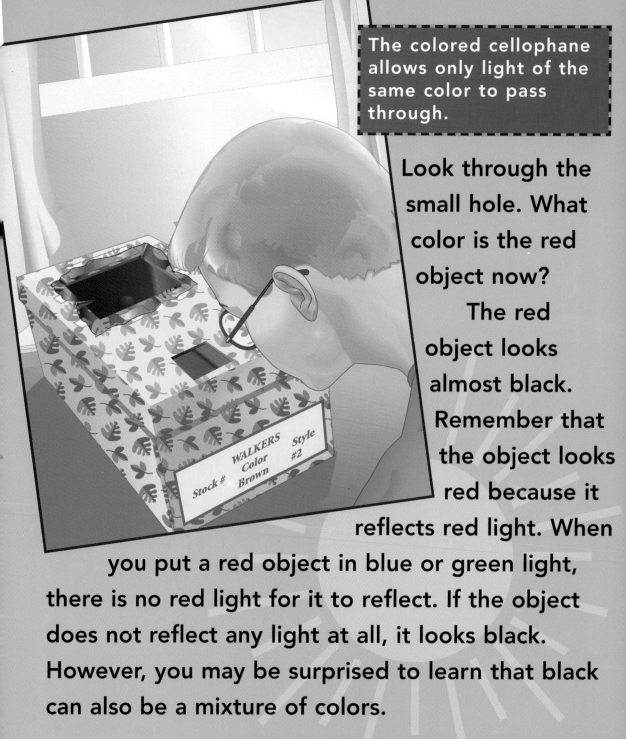

The colored cellophane allows only light of the same color to pass through.

Look through the small hole. What color is the red object now? The red object looks almost black. Remember that the object looks red because it reflects red light. When you put a red object in blue or green light, there is no red light for it to reflect. If the object does not reflect any light at all, it looks black. However, you may be surprised to learn that black can also be a mixture of colors.

WALKERS   Style
Color   #2
Stock #   Brown

Separating the Colors in Black

You will need:
- round coffee filter
- black marker (not permanent)
- ruler
- coffee mug

Flatten the coffee filter. Use the marker and ruler to draw a line across the filter, about 1 inch (2.5 cm) from the bottom. Pour about a 0.25 inch (0.5 cm) of water into the mug. Curl the filter so that the black line is on the outside. Put the filter inside the mug so that the black line is just above the water. Watch the water flow up the filter.

Colors in the
black ink should
start to appear
when the water
reaches the line
you drew on the
coffee filter.

What happens when the
water touches the black line?
When the water reaches the top
of the filter, take the filter out
of the mug. Allow the filter to dry. How many
colors do you see?

28

The black ink in the marker actually contains different colors. Mixing all these colors produces black. Each color is called a **pigment**. As the water travels up the filter, it carries these colored pigments along with it. Because the pigments in black ink travel at different rates, they separate as they move up the paper. Pigments that are smaller and lighter travel up the filter faster. This process of separating the different pigments is called **chromatography**. Now see how colors can be made from just black and white.

Mixing blue, red, and green produces black.

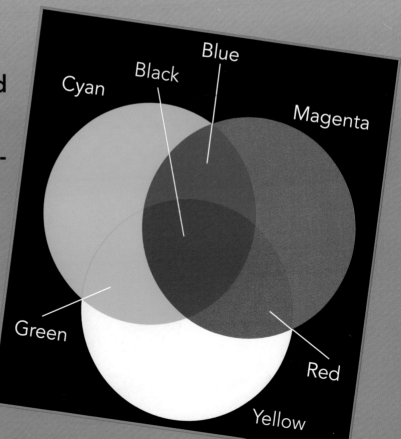

Experiment 6

Turning Black and White Into Color

You will need:
- adult helper
- scissors
- small piece of thick cardboard
- pencil
- glue
- thin nail
- toothpick

Ask an adult to make a photocopy of the black-and-white pattern shown in the circle. Cut out the circle and place it on the cardboard. Trace the circle's outline on the cardboard. Cut out the cardboard circle. Glue the black-and-white pattern to the cardboard circle.

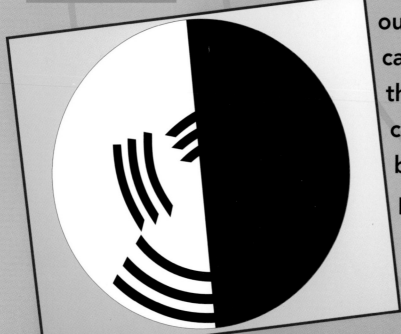

The colors are best seen when the circle spins between five and ten turns per second.

Use the nail to poke a tiny hole through the middle of the circle. Poke the toothpick through the hole. The toothpick should stick out about 0.5 inch (1 cm) on one side. Use a small drop of glue to keep the toothpick in place. Twist the toothpick to spin the circle. Do you see any colors?

The spinning circle is another example of an optical illusion. Scientists are still not sure how this optical illusion fools the eye so that a person sees colors that are not there. Experiment with other designs to see if you can create another black-and-white pattern that tricks the eye into seeing colors.

How Can You Color Things?

Most people like colorful things. They paint the rooms of their homes different colors. They drive cars that are blue, green, red, and other colors. They plant colorful flowers and wear colorful clothes.

At one time, most people wore clothes that were either white or very dark. Only a few people could afford colorful clothes because the **dyes**

used to color them were very expensive. A dye is a substance used to color objects, such as clothes.

In the 1850s, a scientist developed an inexpensive way to make colorful clothes. He prepared a dye to color clothes purple. Soon after, many other dyes became available so that everyone could wear colorful clothes. Learn how you can prepare a dye to color clothes.

Experiment 7

Coloring Fabrics

You will need:
- adult helper
- onion skins
- small pot
- stove
- strainer
- bowl
- kitchen gloves
- piece of white cotton fabric
- paper towel
- soap

Put the onion skins into the pot and cover them with water. Ask an adult to boil them for fifteen minutes. Allow the water to cool. Pour the colored liquid through the strainer into the bowl. Put on the kitchen gloves and dip the cotton fabric into the liquid. Swish the fabric in the liquid for several minutes. Remove the fabric and squeeze it out. Place the fabric on the paper towel to dry. How colorful is the fabric?

Try preparing dyes from other vegetables that are more colorful. You can experiment with beets and red cabbage. What happens when you wash fabrics colored with dyes in soap and water? Now try to make some colorful patterns on paper.

Experiment 8

Printing Colors

You will need:
- small cap
- red, blue, and yellow poster paints
- three small paper cups
- linseed oil
- small paintbrush
- shallow baking pan or tray
- sheets of white paper
- paper towel

Pour a small capful of each poster paint into the paper cups. Keep the colors separate. Add a little linseed oil to each cup. Gently swirl the cups to mix the paint and oil. Fill the baking pan halfway with water.

Dip the brush into one of the colors. Then gently touch the brush to the surface of the water in the pan.

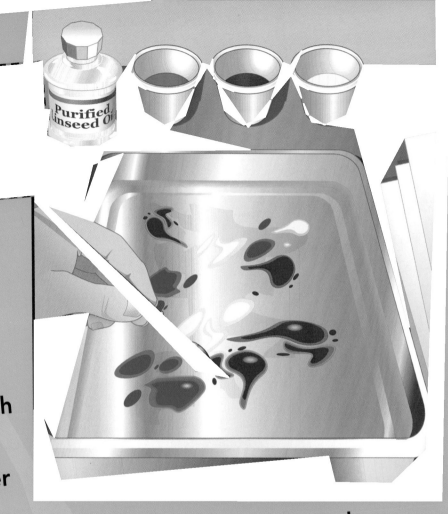

Do the
same with
each of
the other
colors.
Use the brush to swirl the colors around
on the surface of the water.
Carefully lay a sheet of white paper on the
water. After a few seconds, lift the paper from the

water. Place it on the paper towel to dry with the colored surface facing up. Experiment to see what kinds of patterns you can make using different combinations of colors.

The paints stick to the paper where the oil keeps the water from wetting the paper.

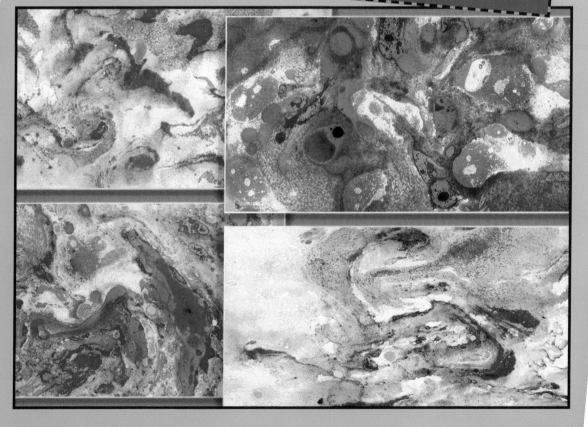

Fun With Colors

Your eyes are sensitive to three colors of light: red, green, and blue. Mixing these colors produces other colors, such as yellow, magenta, and cyan. If red, blue, and green colors of light are mixed equally, you get white. White light is a mixture of the different colors you

can see in a rainbow. Sometimes optical illusions trick your eyes into seeing colors that are not really there. Here's another trick you can play with colors.

Experiment 9

Naming the Colors

You will need:
- helper
- watch or clock with second hand

Look at the words on the opposite page. How quickly can you say aloud the color in which each word is printed? Be sure that you don't say the words that are printed, but the colors in which they are printed.

Most people will start to read the words just as they are written by saying "red, yellow, green...." But you were asked to say the colors in which they are printed. You should say "blue, green, red...." Test family members and friends to see how quickly they can read these

red
yellow
blue
green
yellow
blue
red
red
green
blue

colors according to the instructions. Who can correctly read them the fastest?

Experiment to see if reading a list of ten words correctly is easier if you use non-color words. For example, the first word could be "house" written in red. You would have to say "red" and not "house."

To Find Out More

If you would like to learn more about colors, check out these additional resources.

 **Books**

Ardley, Neil. **Science Book of Color.** Harcourt, 1991.

Baxter, Nicola. **Amazing Colors.** Children's Press, 1995.

Farndon, John. **Color.** Marshall Cavendish, Inc., 2000.

Gold-Dworkin, Heidi. **Exploring Light and Color.** McGraw-Hill Companies, 1999.

Nankivell-Aston, Sally, and Dorothy Jackson. **Science Experiments With Color.** Franklin Watts, 2000.

Nassau, Kurt. **Experimenting With Color.** Franklin Watts, 1997.

Organizations and Online Sites

Cabbage Juice
http://www.howstuffworks.com/experiment1.htm

Mix the juice from red cabbage with various substances you have at home to see what colors you can make. You will also learn about acids and bases.

Catch a Rainbow
http://www.kidzone.ws/science/rainbow.htm

See how you can use red, blue, and yellow food coloring along with some milk to make all the colors of a rainbow.

Exploratorium
3601 Lyon Street
San Francisco, CA 94123
http://www.exploratorium.edu/exhibits/bird_in_a_cage/bird_in_a_cage.html

Visit this site and take a look at the optical illusions.

Fizzing and Foaming
http://scifun.chem.wisc.edu/homeexpts/fizzfoam.html

Learn how you can use a few items that are probably in your kitchen to make a colored liquid that fizzes and foams.

Making Optical Illusion Spinners
http://www.jjlahr.com/science/Illusions/fbkspin.html

This site has links to other black-and-white circles to spin and make colors. Search the Internet for other sites that feature these circles, which are called Benham's disks.

Important Words

chromatography way to separate different pigments that are mixed together

colorblind not able to see certain colors, such as red and green

cones tiny structures in the retina that are sensitive to red, green, and blue light

dye substance that is used to color objects, such as clothes

optical illusion image that looks different from what it really is

pigment colored substance

retina area at the back of the eye where light strikes

Index

Meet the Author

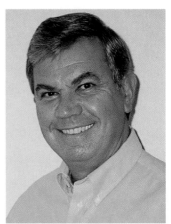

Salvatore Tocci is a science writer who lives in East Hampton, New York, with his wife, Patti. He was a high school biology and chemistry teacher for almost thirty years. As a teacher, he always encouraged his students to perform experiments to learn about science. Every fall, he and his wife travel through New England to see and photograph the colorful foliage.